1 MOVE CHECKMATES

200 INSTRUCTIVE AND CHALLENGING MATES FOR BEGINNERS!

♛

This book is dedicated to Maya and Hakeem and all those just starting out in their journey into the chess world. Each new generation of chess players enriches the great legacy of the Royal Game.

1 MOVE CHECKMATES

200 INSTRUCTIVE AND CHALLENGING MATES FOR BEGINNERS!

ERIC SCHILLER

CARDOZA PUBLISHING

2019 Edition

Copyright © 2005, 2019 by Eric Schiller
- All Rights Reserved -

Library of Congress Catalog Card No: 2018947250
ISBN 13: 978-1-58042-377-9

Visit our web site—www.cardozabooks.com—or write for a full list of books and computer strategies.

CARDOZA PUBLISHING
P.O. Box 98115, Las Vegas, NV 89193
Phone (800) 577-WINS
email: cardozabooks@aol.com
www.cardozabooks.com

CONTENTS

Introduction

The goal of every game of chess is to checkmate your opponent. **Checkmate** takes place when the king is under attack and cannot escape. If the player cannot move his king to any square that is not under attack, cannot capture the checking piece, and cannot block the check by moving some other piece between the attacking piece and the king, then the king is checkmated and the game is over.

Unless your opponent voluntarily resigns, or, if you are playing with a timer, exceeds the agreed-upon time limit, checkmate is the only way to win the game. Even if you capture all of the enemy pieces other than the king, you don't actually win the game until you hunt the king down and checkmate him.

Here is an example of a checkmate:

White to move

The picture, known as a **diagram**, shows four pieces on a chessboard. White has a king, located at the square b1 (the vertical line is the b-file, the horizontal line is the 1st rank). There is a bishop at c2 and a queen at f5. Black's king sits on h8. Since it is White's turn, the queen can move from f5 to h7, placing the enemy king in check.

Black to move

The king cannot run away, and the queen cannot be captured because it is protected by the bishop. So we have a checkmate position, and White wins the game. You can also mate by moving the queen to f8.

When starting out in chess, one of the very first things you have to learn is how to checkmate the enemy king. There are many different checkmating patterns. In the first section of the book, you'll see many of the most common and famous checkmating patterns in action. It isn't necessary to memorize all these patterns, but the more you familiarize yourself with them, the easier it will be to finish off your opponent.

In the second part of the book, you will be challenged to find the checkmating move that was played—or perhaps overlooked—in an actual game situation. These are fairly simple variations on the basic checkmating patterns found in the first section of this book.

The last section of the book contains puzzles that challenge you to find the checkmating move. These are a little more difficult because there are many different checking moves available and in some cases, the checkmating piece comes from far away—perhaps from a region of the battlefield that seems irrelevant. The solutions to these puzzles are found in the back of the book.

After solving all the puzzles in this book, you will be well prepared to deliver checkmate when the opportunity arises. You will learn to anticipate your opponent's checkmating schemes and thwart them. As you gain more chess experience and knowledge, you'll even be able to spot checkmating plans in advance. Eventually, this knowledge will form the foundation for successful chess strategy.

Work through this book at your own pace and enjoy solving these critically important chess positions. If you've just learned the game, it may take you some time to work out the solutions. If you have had some experience playing, you may be able to fly through this book at a fast pace. Even if you are an experienced player, you will probably run into many checkmating patterns that you haven't seen before, and you will sharpen skills that will help you win a lot of games.

After you have completed all of these exercises, you'll be ready to move on to checkmating plans that are two, three, four, or more moves long. You can continue your challenge by exploring books such as *303 Tricky Checkmates* by Fred Wilson and Bruce Alberston, also published by Cardoza.

Basic Checkmating Patterns

This section of this book contains puzzles involving the most basic checkmating patterns. There are thirty-three mates for you to solve with the solutions to them in the back of the book. The first diagram reveals the fastest possible mate in chess. See if you can find the move.

1.
FOOL'S MATE

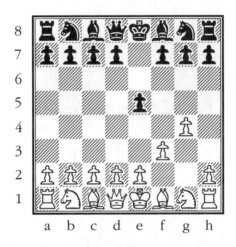

Black to move

2.
BACK RANK MATE

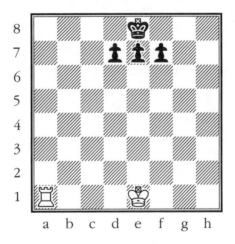

White to move

1 MOVE CHECKMATES

3.
ANASTASIA'S MATE

White to move

4.
ANDERSSEN'S MATE

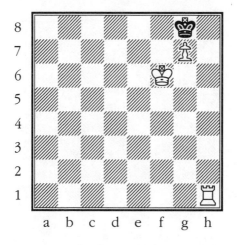

White to move

5.
ARABIAN MATE

White to move

6.
BLACKBURNE'S MATE

White to move

7.
BODEN'S MATE

White to move

8.
DAMIANO'S MATE

White to move

9.
CORNER MATE

White to move

10.
COZIO'S MATE

White to move

1 MOVE CHECKMATES

11.
DAMIANO'S BISHOP MATE

White to move

12.
DAVID AND GOLIATH MATE

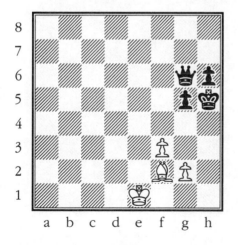

White to move

13.
DOUBLE BISHOP MATE

White to move

14.
DOVETAIL MATE

White to move

1 MOVE CHECKMATES

15.
EPAULETTE MATE

White to move

16.
GRECO'S MATE

White to move

17.
HOOK MATE

White to move

18.
"H" FILE MATE

White to move

1 MOVE CHECKMATES

19.
LEGALL'S MATE

White to move

20.
LOLLI'S MATE

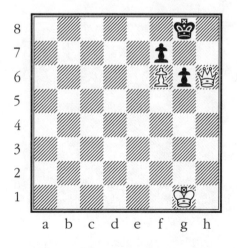

White to move

21.
MAX LANGE'S MATE

White to move

22.
MINOR PIECE MATE

White to move

23.
MORPHY'S MATE

White to move

24.
RETI'S MATE

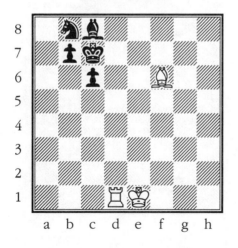

White to move

25.
MORPHY'S OPERA HOUSE MATE

White to move

26.
PILLSBURY'S MATE

White to move

27.
QUEEN AND PAWN MATE

White to move

28.
SMOTHERED MATE

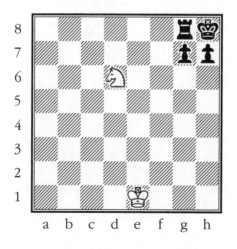

White to move

29.
SUFFOCATION MATE

White to move

30.
SWALLOWTAIL MATE

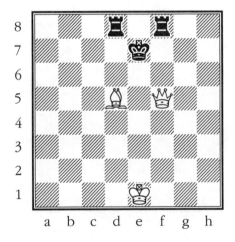

White to move

31.
ROLLER OR STAIRCASE MATE

White to move

32.
SCHOLAR'S MATE

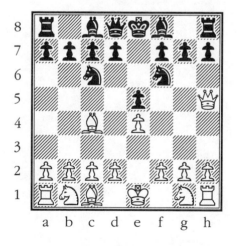

White to move

33.
QUEEN'S CORNER MATE

White to move

Simple Checkmates

Now that you've seen the basic checkmating patterns, try to apply your knowledge to find the move that gives checkmate in each of the following positions. The checkmating move must give check to the enemy king, of course, but remember that not all moves that give check are checkmate. Make sure that the move you choose not only puts the enemy king in check, but also prevents the enemy from capturing the checking piece, blocking the check by putting something in the way, or running away to a safe square.

34.

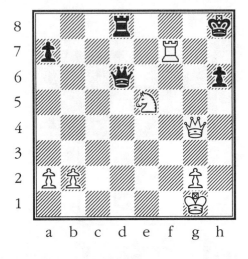

White to move

35.

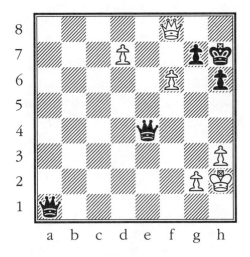

White to move

36.

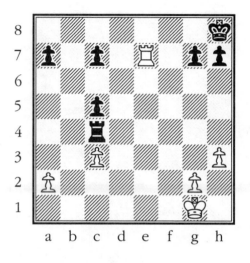

White to move

37.

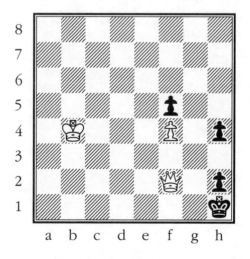

White to move

38.

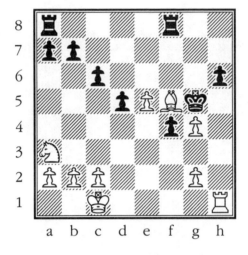

White to move

39.

White to move

40.

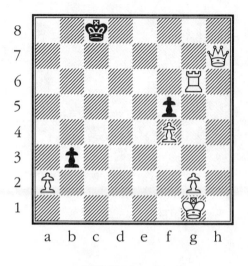

White to move

41.

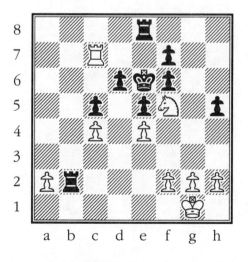

White to move

42.

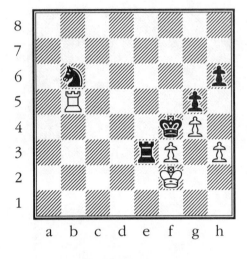

White to move

43.

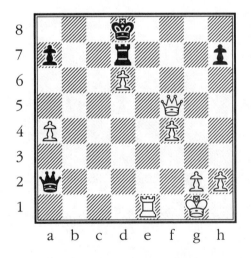

White to move

44.

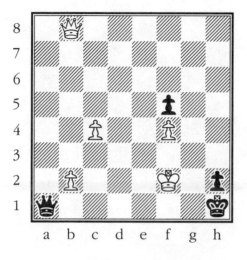

White to move

45.

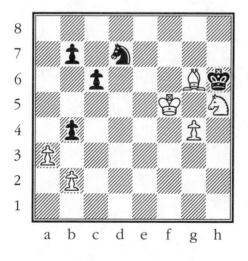

White to move

46.

White to move

47.

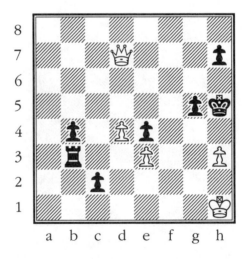

White to move

48.

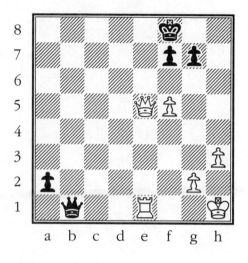

White to move

49.

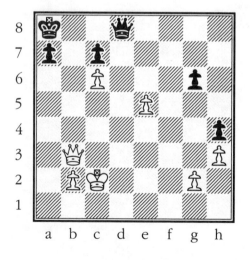

White to move

50.

White to move

51.

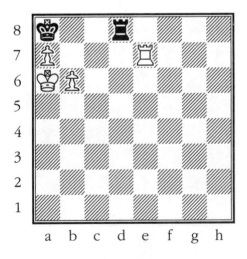

White to move

52.

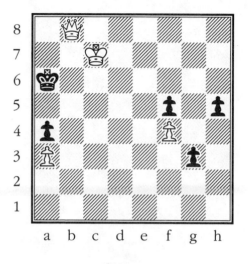

White to move

53.

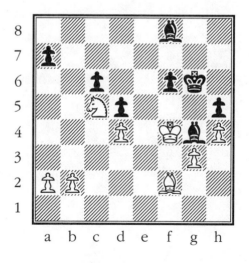

Black to move

54.

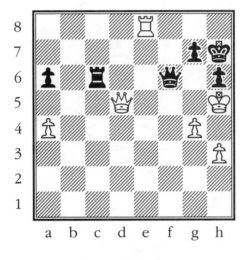

White to move

55.

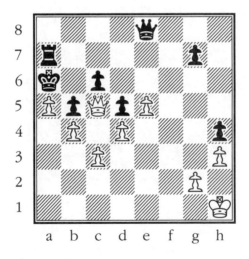

White to move

56.

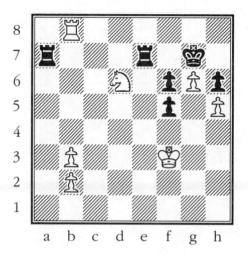

White to move

57.

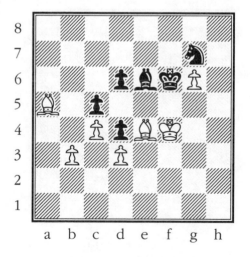

White to move

58.

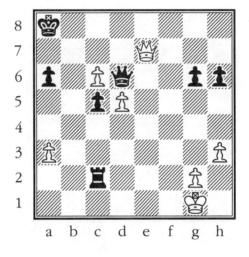

White to move

59.

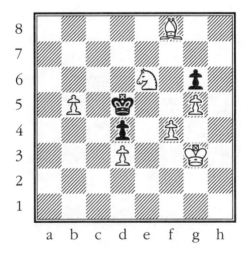

White to move

60.

White to move

61.

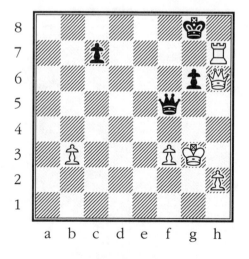

White to move

62.

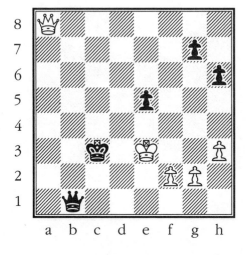

Black to move

63.

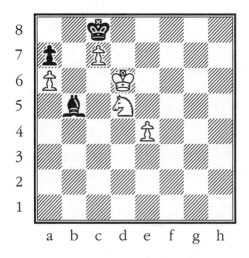

White to move

64.

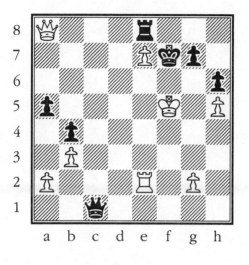

White to move

65.

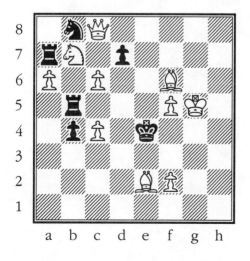

White to move

66.

White to move

67.

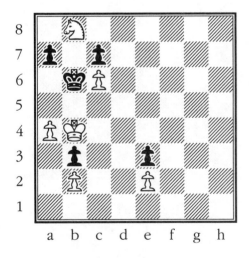

White to move

68.

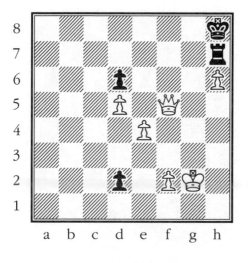

White to move

69.

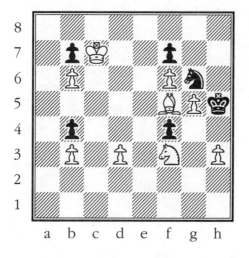

White to move

70.

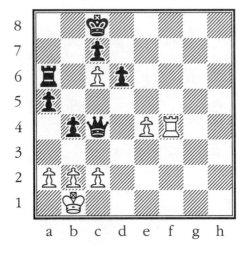

White to move

71.

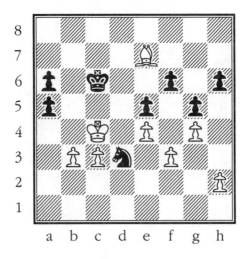

Black to move

72.

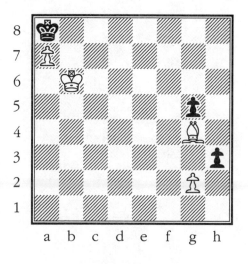

White to move

73.

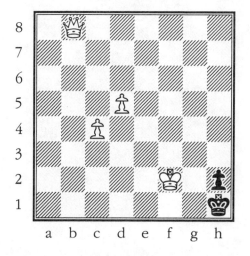

White to move

74.

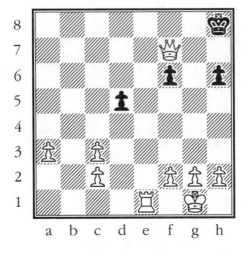

White to move

75.

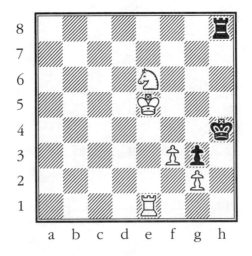

White to move

76.

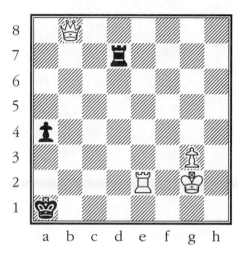

White to move

77.

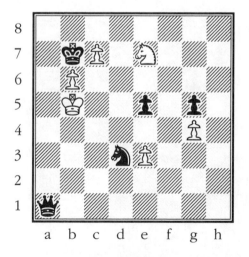

White to move

78.

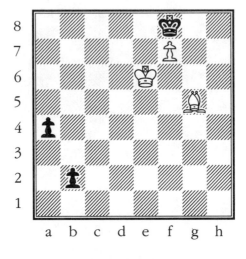

White to move

79.

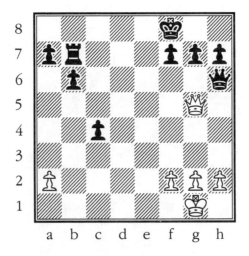

White to move

80.

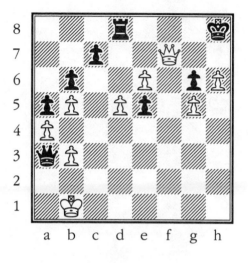

White to move

81.

White to move

82.

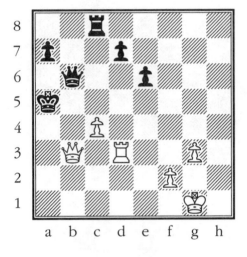

White to move

83.

White to move

84.

White to move

85.

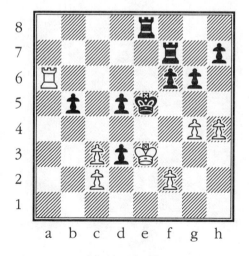

White to move

86.

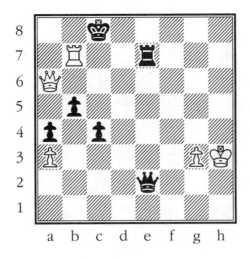

White to move

87.

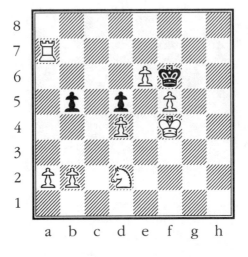

White to move

88.

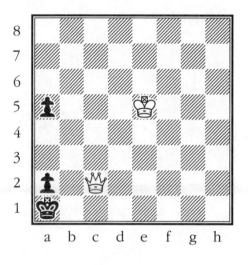

White to move

89.

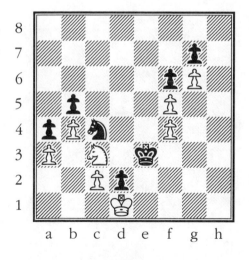

Black to move

90.

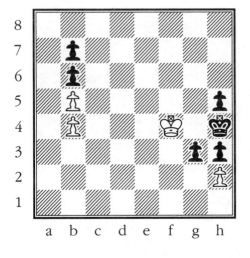

White to move

91.

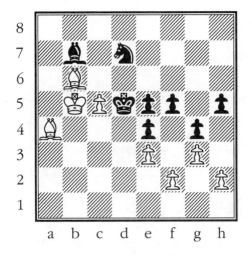

White to move

92.

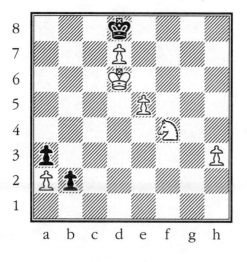

White to move

93.

White to move

94.

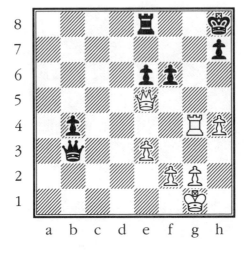

White to move

95.

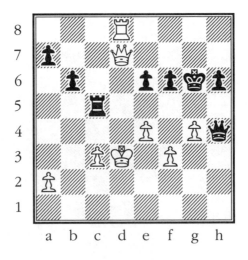

White to move

96.

White to move

97.

White to move

98.

White to move

99.

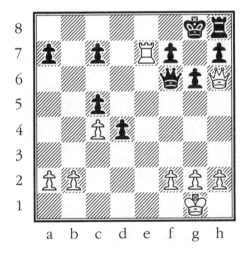

White to move

100.

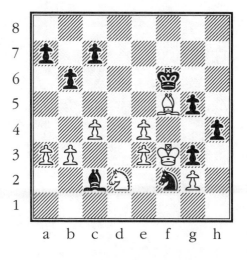

Black to move

101.

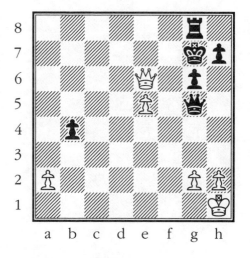

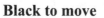

Black to move

102.

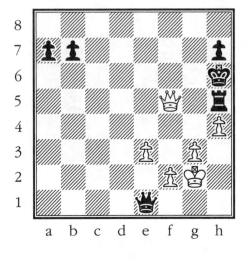

White to move

103.

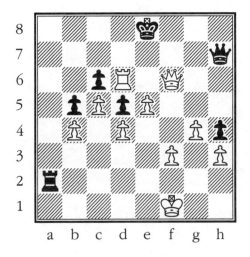

Black to move

104.

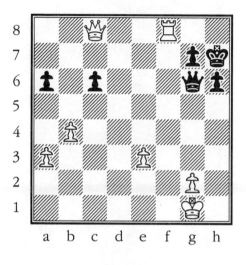

White to move

105.

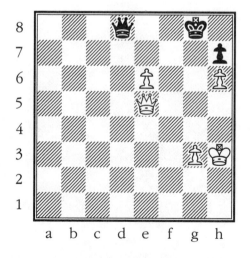

White to move

106.

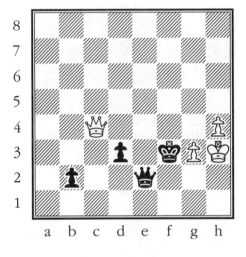

White to move

107.

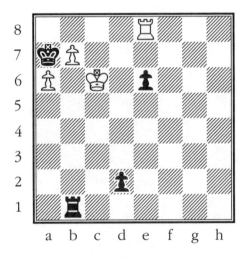

White to move

108.

White to move

109.

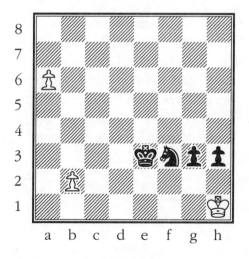

Black to move

More Challenging
Checkmates

Now that you've mastered the material in the first two sections of the book, the rest of these checkmates shouldn't be too difficult to figure out. They are a bit more challenging, however, so watch out for moves that come from an unusual direction or from all the way across the board. In some cases, the checkmating move will also involve protecting one of the pieces that is being attacked by your opponent's king. These positions often have multiple checking options, so make sure you find the right one!

110.

White to move

111.

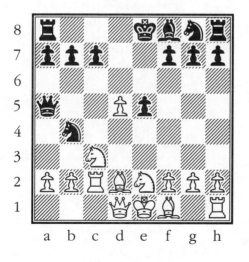

Black to move

112.

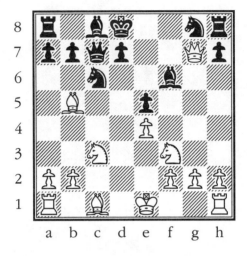

White to move

113.

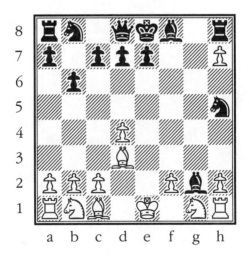

White to move

114.

White to move

115.

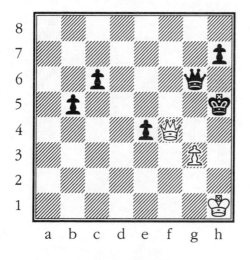

White to move

116.

White to move

117.

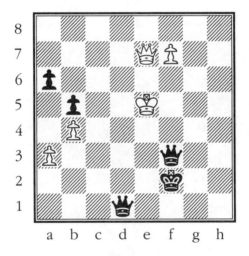

Black to move

1 MOVE CHECKMATES

118.

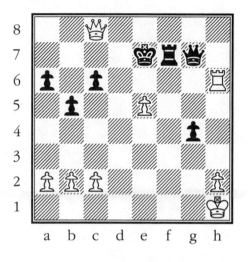

White to move

119.

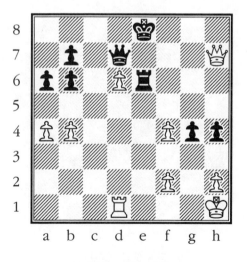

White to move

120.

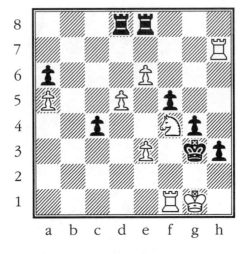

White to move

121.

Black to move

122.

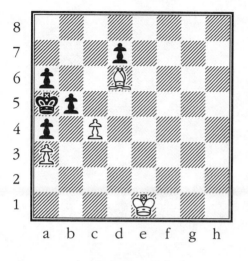

White to move

123.

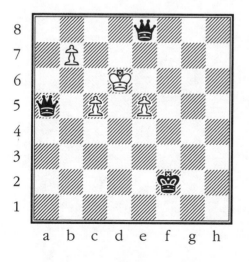

Black to move

124.

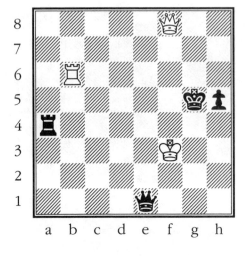

White to move

125.

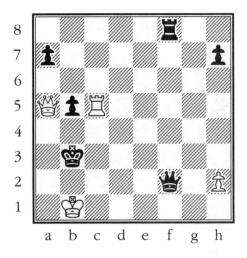

White to move

126.

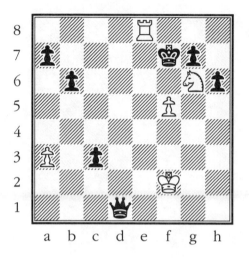

White to move

127.

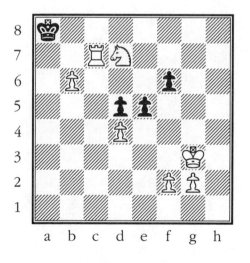

White to move

128.

White to move

129.

White to move

130.

White to move

131.

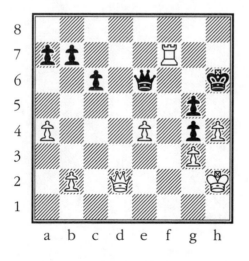

White to move

132.

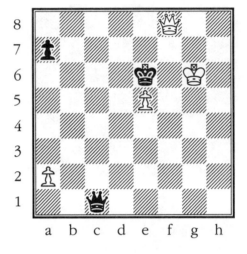

White to move

133.

White to move

134.

Black to move

135.

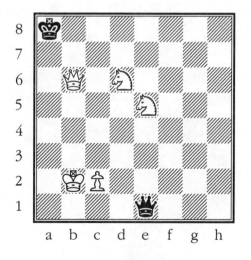

White to move

136.

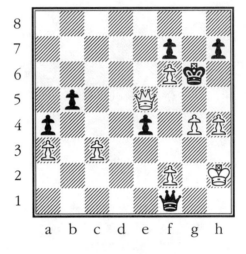

White to move

137.

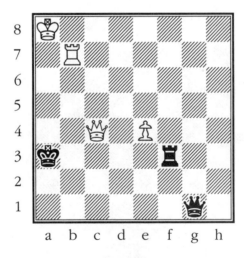

White to move

138.

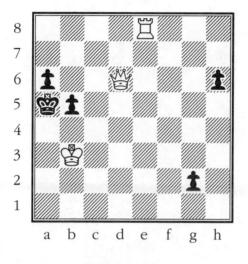

White to move

139.

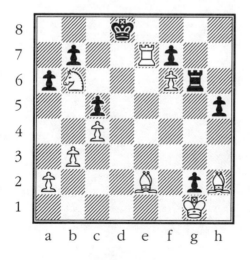

White to move

140.

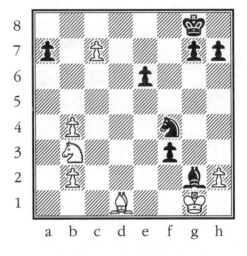

Black to move

141.

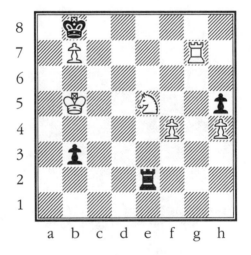

White to move

142.

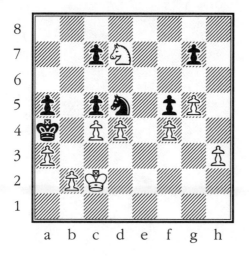

White to move

143.

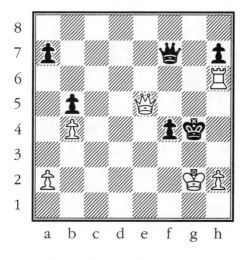

White to move

144.

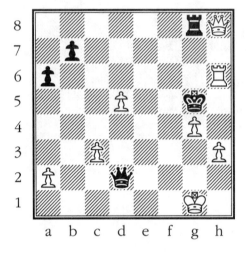

White to move

145.

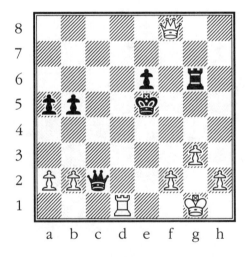

White to move

146.

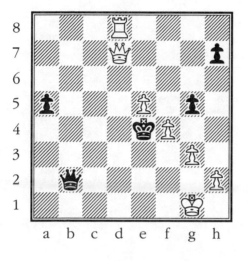

White to move

147.

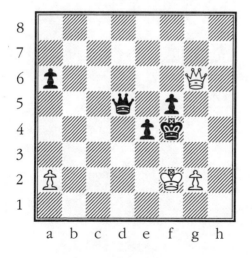

White to move

148.

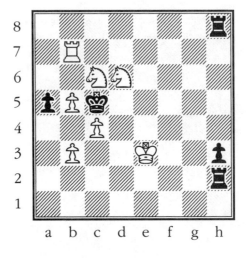

White to move

149.

White to move

150.

White to move

151.

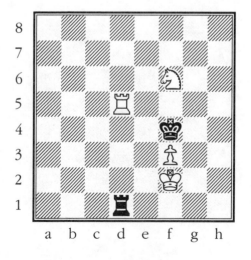

White to move

152.

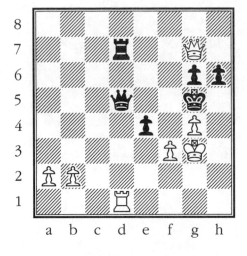

White to move

153.

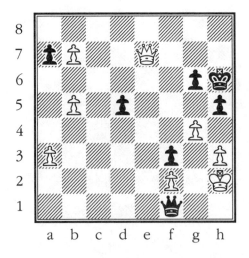

White to move

1 MOVE CHECKMATES

154.

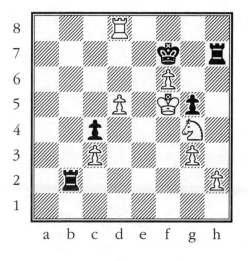

White to move

155.

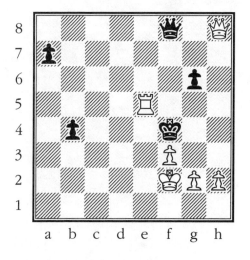

White to move

156.

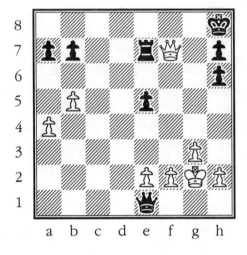

White to move

157.

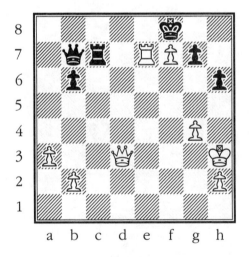

White to move

158.

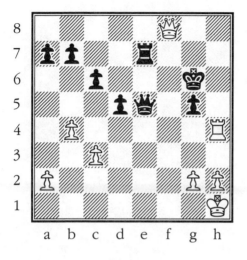

White to move

159.

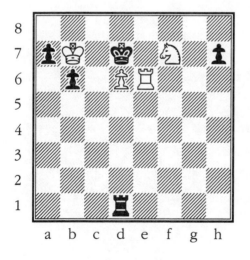

White to move

160.

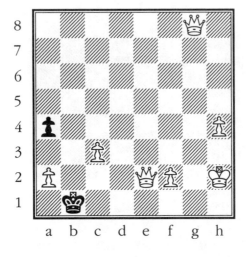

White to move

161.

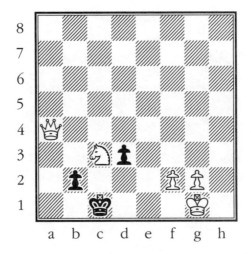

White to move

162.

Black to move

163.

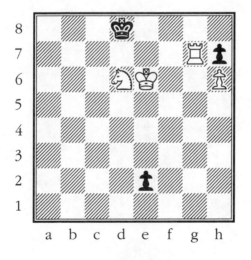

White to move

164.

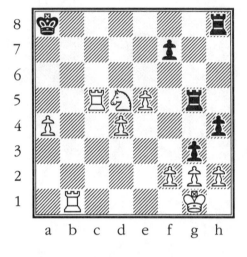

White to move

165.

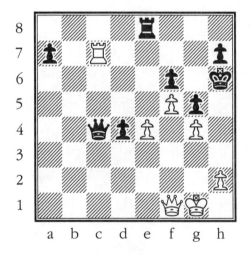

White to move

166.

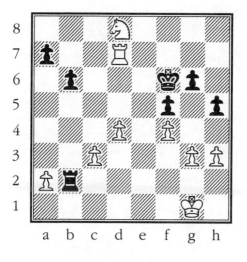

White to move

167.

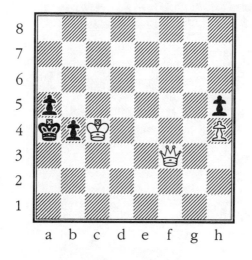

White to move

168.

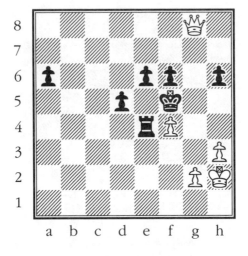

White to move

169.

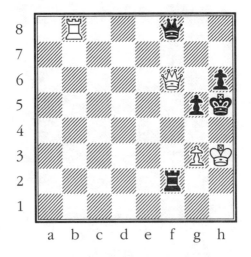

White to move

Still More Challenging Checkmates

170.

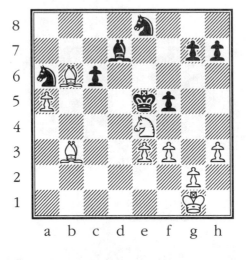

White to move

171.

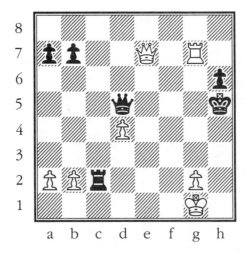

White to move

1 MOVE CHECKMATES

172.

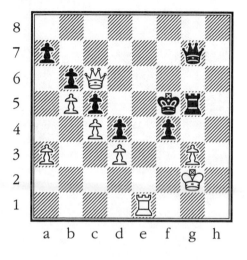

White to move

173.

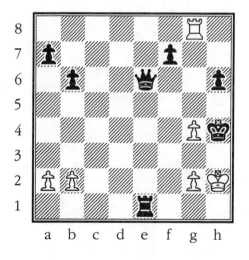

White to move

174.

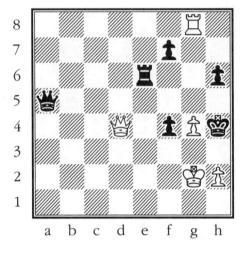

White to move

175.

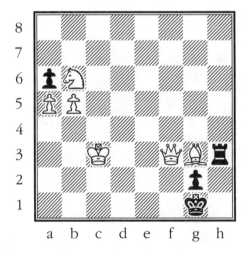

White to move

176.

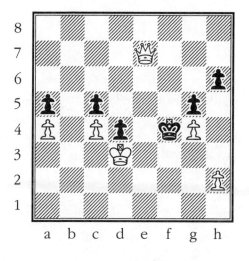

White to move

177.

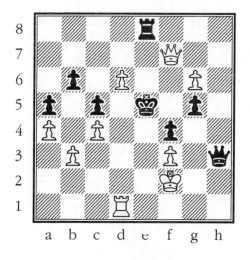

White to move

178.

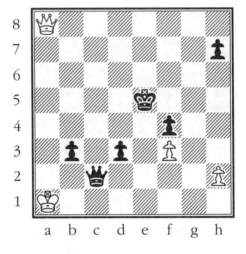

Black to move

179.

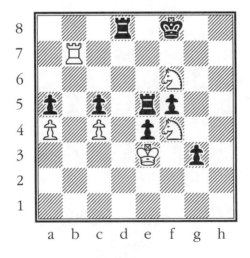

White to move

I MOVE CHECKMATES

180.

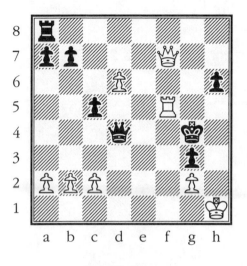

White to move

181.

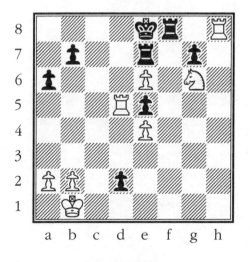

White to move

182.

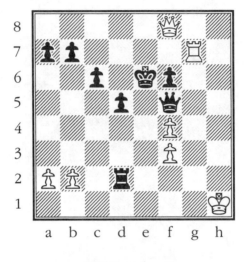

White to move

183.

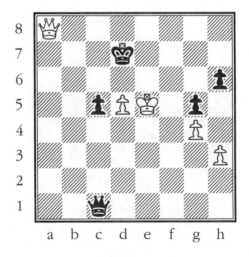

Black to move

184.

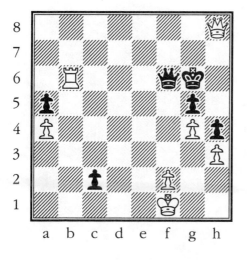

White to move

185.

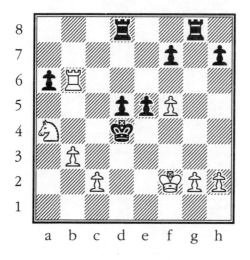

White to move

186.

White to move

187.

White to move

188.

White to move

189.

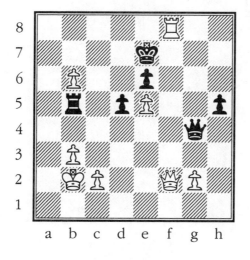

White to move

190.

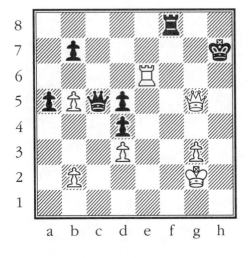

White to move

191.

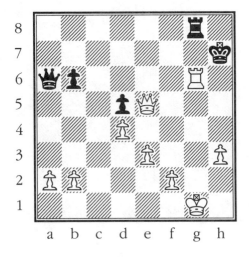

White to move

1 MOVE CHECKMATES

192.

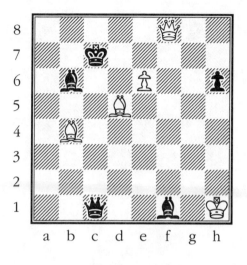

White to move

193.

White to move

194.

White to move

195.

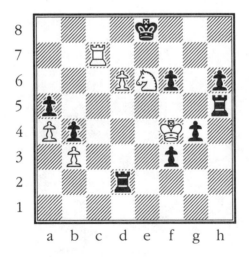

White to move

196.

White to move

197.

White to move

198.

White to move

199.

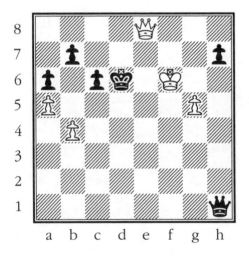

White to move

200.

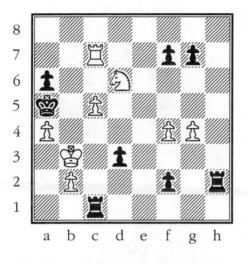

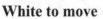

White to move

Puzzle Solutions

1 MOVE CHECKMATES

1) 1...Qh4#

5) 1.Rh7#

2) 1.Ra8#

6) 1.Bh7#

3) 1.Rh5#

7) 1.Ba6#

4) 1.Rh8#

8) 1.Qh7#

9) 1.Nf7#

13) 1.Bd4#

10) 1.Qh2#

14) 1.Qf6#

11) 1.Qg7#

15) 1.Qe6#

12) 1.g4#

16) 1.Qh5#

1 MOVE CHECKMATES

17) 1.Re8#

21) 1.Qg8#

18) 1.Rh8#

22) 1.Bd5#

19) 1.Nd5#

23) 1.Be5#

20) 1.Qg7#

24) 1.Bd8#

25) 1.Rd8#

29) 1.Ne7#

26) 1.Rg1#

30) 1.Qe6#

27) 1.Qg7#

31) 1.Qh4#

28) 1.Nf7#

32) 4.Qxf7#

1 MOVE CHECKMATES

33) 1.Qf8#

37) 1.Qf1#

34) 1.Qg7#

38) 1.Rh5#

35) 1.Qxg7#

39) 1.Rh7#

36) 1.Re8#

40) 1.Rg8#

41) 1.Ng7#

45) 1.g5#

42) 1.Rf5#

46) 1.Qh6#

43) 1.Qf8#

47) 1.Qxh7#

44) 1.Qb7#

48) 1.Qe8#

I MOVE CHECKMATES

49) 1.Qb7#

53) 1...Bh6#

50) 1.Qc2#

54) 1.Qg8#

51) 1.b7#

55) 1.Qb6#

52) 1.Qb6#

56) 1.Nxf5#

57) 1.Bd8#

61) 1.Qg7#

58) 1.Qb7#

62) 1...Qd3#

59) 1.Nc7#

63) 1.Ne7#

60) 1.Qf2#

64) 1.Qd5#

1 MOVE CHECKMATES

65) 1.Nd6#

69) 1.Bg4#

66) 1.Nb6#

70) 1.Rf8#

67) 1.a5#

71) 1...Nb2#

68) 1.Qf8#

72) 1.Bf3#

73) 1.Qb1#

77) 1.c8=Q#

74) 1.Re8#

78) 1.Bh6#

75) 1.Rh1#

79) 1.Qd8#

76) 1.Qb2#

80) 1.Qg7#

1 MOVE CHECKMATES

81) 1.Qh8#

85) 1.f4#

82) 1.Qa3#

86) 1.Rf7#

83) 1.Qf7#

87) 1.Qa8#

84) 1.Qh5#

88) 1.Qc1#

89) 1...Nb2#

93) 1.e7#

90) 1.hxg3#

94) 1.Qxf6#

91) 1.Bb3#

95) 1.Rg8#

92) 1.Ne6#

96) 1.Qxf5#

1 MOVE CHECKMATES

97) 1.Rh8#

101) 1...Qc1#

98) 1.f7#

102) 1.Qf6#

99) 1.Re8#

103) 1...Qb1#

100) 1...Bd1#

104) 1.Rh8#

105) 1.Qg7#

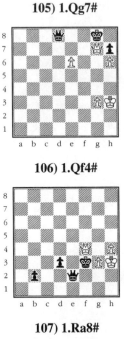

109) 1...g2#

106) 1.Qf4#

110) 1.Qe6#

107) 1.Ra8#

111) 1...Nd3#

108) 1.Nc2#

112) 1.Qf8#

1 MOVE CHECKMATES

113) 1.Bg6#

117) 1...Qdd5#

114) 1.Nc6#

118) 1.Re6#

115) 1.Qh4#

119) 1.Qg8#

116) 1.Rf7#

120) 1.Ne2#

121) 1...Qdd6#

125) 1.Rc3#

122) 1.Bc7#

126) 1.Rf8#

123) 1...Qad8#

127) 1.Ra7#

124) 1.Qf6#

128) 1.Qa4#

1 MOVE CHECKMATES

129) 1.Qf5#

133) 1.Rb6#

130) 1.Qe7#

134) 1...Qh1#

131) 1.Qxg5#

135) 1.Qb7#

132) 1.Qd6#

136) 1.Qg5#

137) 1.Qa6#

141) 1.Nc6#

138) 1.Qc7#

142) 1.Nxc5#

139) 1.Bc7#

143) 1.h3#

140) 1...Nh3#

144) 1.Qf6#

1 MOVE CHECKMATES

145) 1.Qf4#

149) 1.Rg7#

146) 1.Qd3#

150) 1.Qxh4#

147) 1.Qg3#

151) 1.Nh5#

148) 1.Ne4#

152) 1.f4#

153) 1.g5#

157) 1.Qd8#

154) 1.Ne5#

158) 1.Rh6#

155) 1.g3#

159) 1.Re7#

156) 1.Qf8#

160) 1.Qg1#

1 MOVE CHECKMATES

161) 1.Qd1#

165) 1.Qh3#

162) 1...Qd3#

166) 1.Rf7#

163) 1.Rd7#

167) 1.Qb3#

164) 1.Ra5#

168) 1.Qg4#

169) 1.g4#

173) 1.g3#

170) 1.Bd4#

174) 1.Qf2#

171) 1.g4#

175) 1.Qd1#

172) 1.Qe6#

176) 1.Qe4#

1 MOVE CHECKMATES

177) 1.Rd5#

181) 1.Rxf8#

178) 1...Qc1#

182) 1.Qe7#

179) 1.Ng6#

183) 1...Qf4#

180) 1.Qh5#

184) 1.Rxf6#

185) 1.Rb4#

189) 1.Qf7#

186) 1.Kf2#

190) 1.Rh6#

187) 1.Nhg6#

191) 1.Qh5#

188) 1.Ngf7#

192) 1.Bd6#

1 MOVE CHECKMATES

193) 1.Nf3#

197) 1.Rh7#

194) 1.Bxg3#

198) 1.Rh5#

195) 1.Re7#

199) 1.Qd8#

196) 1.Nb6#

200) 1.Nb7#

Basics of
Chess Notation

We refer to the horizontal rows as ranks and the vertical columns as files. The ranks are numbered 1-8, from White's point of view. The files are designated by letters, from a-h. The pieces have the following abbreviations: king is K; queen is Q; rook is R; bishop is B; knight is N (not K, because that is reserved for the king). The pawn has no abbreviation, but as long as there is no other capital letter indicated, then we understand that it must be a pawn move. After the abbreviation for the piece, the square the piece lands on is usually indicated next.

Our first move is pushing the king pawn two squares forward. We write, **1.e4**. The position after the move is shown below:

Now suppose we want to describe Black's reply, also moving the pawn on the kingside to a position two squares in front of the king. This move would be written **1...e5**. We use an ellipsis (…) to indicate that it is not White's move, but Black's. If we want to describe the entire game so far, we write simply 1.e4 e5. In this instance, we didn't use the ellipsis, since the White and Black moves are represented together. As you can see, the White move is always shown first, then the Black move after.

Now let's say that White brings the bishop to b5. That move is written **2.Bb5.** The "2" indicates White's second move, the Bb5 shows that a bishop has moved to the b5 square. The game now reads 1.e4 e5; 2.Bb5.

Black responds by bringing a knight to c6. We notate that as **2... Nc6**. We don't have to say which knight, because only one of the Black knights can move to c6.

White goes **3.Nf3** and black replies **3...a6**. Now let us introduce a new element. We will capture the knight with our bishop. Because we are capturing an enemy piece, we add an "x" between the piece and a capture. We represent the move with **4.Bxc6.** Annotation of the game so far would be as follows: 1.e4 e5; 2.Bb5 Nc6; 3.Nf3 a6; 4.Bxc6.

Black's pawn takes the bishop. Because we need to clarify which of the two possible pawn captures occured, we add the file that the pawn is leaving from: **4...dxc6**. We see that it is the pawn on the d-file that is making the capture, not the pawn on the b-file.

Now White castles. There is a simple convention to show this. We use two zeros separated by a hyphen to indicate castling on the kingside (castling short): **5.0-0**. For queenside castling, we would add another hyphen and another zero "0-0-0".

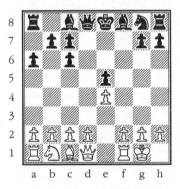

A few final points. If you put the enemy king in check, you indicate this by appending a suffix in the form of a plus "+" sign, for example Qh5+. If it was an actual checkmate, it will be indicated by "#".

One final point. If you are lucky enough to promote a pawn into a queen, it is written by marking the square that the pawn promotes onto, affixing an equal "=" sign, and then indicating the piece the pawn is promoted to. For example, e8=Q means that the pawn moves to the e8 square and is replaced by a queen.

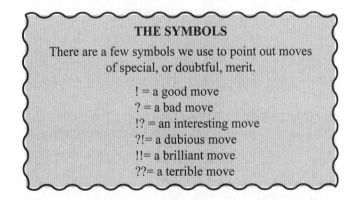

THE SYMBOLS

There are a few symbols we use to point out moves
of special, or doubtful, merit.

! = a good move
? = a bad move
!? = an interesting move
?!= a dubious move
!!= a brilliant move
??= a terrible move